Saint Joseph

GUIDE

FOR

Christian Prayer

(The Liturgy of the Hours)

For use with Edition No. 406

2022

No. 406/G

CATHOLIC BOOK PUBLISHING CORP.

New Jersey

catholicbookpublishing.com

The purpose of this handy GUIDE is to facilitate use of CHRISTIAN PRAYER, the one-volume **Liturgy of the Hours**, by providing clear, accurate references for each day of the year—always in accord with the principles on which this particular Breviary was compiled. These principles are enunciated on pages 34-37 of the volume and the use of this GUIDE is dependent upon a thorough understanding of these directives. Whenever a Saint is celebrated as a Memorial, the numbers in parentheses refer to the page in the Common that is to be used; the numbers without parentheses refer to the page in the Psalter that is to be used. (See p. 37 under Memorials.)

The designation **(New)** indicates that the Saint in question is found in the revised **SUPPLEMENT of the Liturgy of the Hours** (No. 405/04) published in 1992. **(No SUPPLEMENT has been approved for publication since that time.).** The designation *(New)* in lightface italics indicates that the Saint in question must be taken from the pertinent Common.

For those who will use the Edition with Music and the Office of Readings, the pertinent information is supplied on a separate line within brackets at the end of each entry.

LIST OF ABBREVIATIONS

Ab — Abbot
Ant — Antiphon
Ap — Apostle
B, Bb — Bishop(s)
Bl. — Blessed
BVM — Blessed Virgin Mary
Comp(s) — Companion(s)
D, Dd — Doctor(s)
De — Deacon
Ded — Dedication of Church
DP — Daytime Prayer
EP — Evening Prayer
F — Feast
f — following page(s)
M, Mm — Martyr(s)

Mem — Memorial (Obligatory)
Miss — Missionaries
MP — Morning Prayer
NP — Night Prayer
OOR — Office of Readings
P, Pp — Priest(s)
Po — Pope
Pr — Prayer
Rd — Reading(s)
Rel — Religious
Sol — Solemnity
St., Sts. — Saint(s)
TD — Te Deum
V — Virgin

(406/G)

© 2021 Catholic Book Publishing Corp., N.J.
Printed in the U.S.A.

catholicbookpublishing.com

JANUARY

EP 173 (1368); NP 1034 or 1037

1. **Sat. MARY, MOTHER OF GOD (Sol) 175**
   MP 175 (707); DP 1027; EP 178; NP 1037
   [OOR 1802, Rd 1882f & 1951f; TD Pr 175]

2. **Sun. EPIPHANY (Sol) 211**
   MP 211 (707); DP 1027; EP 214; NP 1037
   [OOR 1806, Rd 1882f & 1965f; TD Pr 211]

3. Mon. Monday after Epiphany or Most Holy Name of Jesus *(New)*
   No official texts exist yet in English.
   MP (218) 792; DP 998; EP (220) 798; NP 1041
   [OOR 1809, Rd 1882f & 1955f; Pr 221]

4. Tue. St. Elizabeth Ann Seton (Mem) 1061
   MP (1470) 802; DP 1003; EP (1471) 807; NP 1044
   [OOR 1812, Rd 1882f & 2049f; Pr 1061]

5. Wed. St. John Neumann, B (Mem) 1062
   MP (1426) 812; DP 1008; EP (1430) 818; NP 1046
   [OOR 1816, Rd 1882f & 2046f; Pr 1062]

6. Thu. Thursday after Epiphany or St. André Bessette, Rel **(New)** (5)
   MP (228) (1470) 824 Pr proper (6) or 1471; DP 1012
   EP (229) (1471) 830 Pr (6) or 1471; NP 1049
   [OOR 1819, Rd 1882f & 1955f or 2049f; Pr (6) or 1471 or 229]

7. Fri. Friday after Epiphany or St. Raymond of Penyafort, P (1063)
   MP (231) (1426) 835; DP 1017; EP (233) (1430) 840; NP 1052
   [OOR 1821, Rd 1882f & 1955f or 2046f; Pr 1063 or 233]

8. Sat. Saturday after Epiphany
   MP (235) 845; DP 1022; EP (237) 207; NP 1034
   [OOR 1824, Rd 1882f & 1955f; Pr 236]

9. **Sun. BAPTISM OF THE LORD (F) 239**
   MP (239) 707; DP 994; EP 242 (214); NP 1037
   [OOR 1827, Rd 1882f & 1966f; TD Pr 241]

10. Mon. Monday of the 1st Week in Ordinary Time
    MP 718; DP 998; EP 723; NP 1041
    [OOR 1788, Rd 1924f & 2011f; Pr 245]

11. Tue. Tuesday of the 1st Week in Ordinary Time
MP 728; DP 1003; EP 734; NP 1044
[OOR 1791, Rd 1924f & 2011f; Pr 245]

12. Wed. Wednesday of the 1st Week in Ordinary Time
MP 738; DP 1008; EP 743; NP 1046
[OOR 1794, Rd 1924f & 2011f; Pr 245]

13. Thu. Weekday or St. Hilary, B & D (1063)
MP (1426 or 1435) 748; DP 1012; EP (1430 or 1436) 754; NP 1049
[OOR 1797, Rd 1924f & 2011f or 2046f; Pr 1064 or 245]

14. Fri. Friday of the 1st Week in Ordinary Time
MP 759; DP 1017; EP 765; NP 1052
[OOR 1800, Rd 1924f & 2011f; Pr 245]

15. Sat. Weekday or BVM on Saturday (1383)
MP (1383) 770; DP 1022; EP (246) 775; NP 1034
[OOR 1802, Rd 1924f & 2011f or 1951f; Pr 1386 or 245]

16. **Sun. SECOND SUNDAY IN ORDINARY TIME 246**
MP 780; DP 994; EP 786; NP 1037
[OOR 1806, Rd 1924f & 2011f; TD Pr 246]

17. Mon. St. Anthony, Ab (Mem) 1064
MP (1470) 792; DP 998; EP (1471) 798; NP 1041
[OOR 1809, Rd 1924f & 2049f; Pr 1064]

18. Tue. Tuesday of the 2nd Week in Ordinary Time
MP 802; DP 1003; EP 807; NP 1044
[OOR 1812, Rd 1924f & 2011f; Pr 246]

19. Wed. Wednesday of the 2nd Week in Ordinary Time
MP 812; DP 1008; EP 818; NP 1046
[OOR 1816, Rd 1924f & 2011f; Pr 246]

20. Thu. Weekday or St. Fabian, Po & M, or St. Sebastian, M (1065)
MP (1414 or 1426) 824; DP 1012
EP (1417 or 1430) 830; NP 1049
[OOR 1819, Rd 1924f & 2011f or 2045f; Pr 1065 or 246]

21. Fri. St. Agnes, V & M (Mem) 1065
MP 1066 (707); DP 1017; EP 1067 (1418); NP 1052
[OOR 1821, Rd 1924f & 2045f or 2048f; Pr 1067]

22. Sat. Day of Prayer for the Legal Protection of Unborn Children
    MP 845; DP 1022; EP 851; NP 1034
    [OOR 1824, Rd 1924f & 2011f; Pr 246]

23. **Sun. THIRD SUNDAY IN ORDINARY TIME 247**
    MP 856; DP 994; EP 861; NP 1037
    [OOR 1827, Rd 1924f & 2011f; TD Pr 247]

24. Mon. St. Francis de Sales, B & D (Mem) 1068
    MP (1426 or 1435) 867; DP 998; EP (1430 or 1436) 872; NP 1041
    [OOR 1829, Rd 1924f & 2046f; Pr 1069]

25. Tue. CONVERSION OF ST. PAUL, AP (F) 1069
    MP 1069 (707); DP 1003; EP 1071 (1394); NP 1044
    [OOR 1831, Rd 1924f & 2043f; TD Pr 1071]

26. Wed. Sts. Timothy and Titus, Bb (Mem) 1073
    MP (1426) (Ant) 886; DP 1008; EP (1430) (Ant) 892; NP 1046
    [OOR 1835, Rd 1924f & 2046f; Pr 1073]

27. Thu. Weekday or St. Angela Merici, V (1074)
    MP (1441 or 1473) 897; DP 1012; EP (1444 or 1473) 901; NP 1049
    [OOR 1838, Rd 1924f & 2011f or 2048f; Pr 1074 or 247]

28. Fri. St. Thomas Aquinas, P & D (Mem) 1075
    MP (1435) (Ant) 906; DP 1017; EP (1436) (Ant) 911; NP 1052
    [OOR 1842, Rd 1924f & 2046f; Pr 1075]

29. Sat. Weekday or BVM on Saturday (1383)
    MP (1383) 916; DP 1022; EP 921 (248); NP 1034
    [OOR 1845, Rd 1924f & 2011f or 1951f; Pr 1386 or 247]

30. **Sun. FOURTH SUNDAY IN ORDINARY TIME 248**
    MP 925; DP 994; EP 931; NP 1037
    [OOR 1850, Rd 1924f & 2011f; TD Pr 248]

31. Mon. St. John Bosco, P (Mem) 1076
    MP (1426 or 1473) 937; DP 998; EP (1430 or 1473) 942; NP 1041
    [OOR 1853, Rd 1924f & 2046f; Pr 1076]

FEBRUARY

1. Tue. Tuesday of the 4th Week in Ordinary Time
   MP 947; DP 1003; EP 953; NP 1044
   [OOR 1856, Rd 1924f & 2011f; Pr 248]

2. Wed. PRESENTATION OF THE LORD (F) 1081
MP 1081 (707); DP 1008; EP 1082; NP 1046
[OOR 1859, Rd 1924f & 2011f; TD Pr 1082]

3. Thu. Weekday or St. Blase, B & M (1086) or St. Ansgar, B (1087)
MP (1414 or 1426) 968; DP 1012
EP (1417 or 1430) 973; NP 1049
[OOR 1861, Rd 1924f & 2011f or 2045f or 2046f; Pr 1086 or 1087 or 248]

4. Fri. Friday of the 4th Week in Ordinary Time
MP 978; DP 1017; EP 984; NP 1052
[OOR 1864, Rd 1924f & 2011f; Pr 248]

5. Sat. St. Agatha, V & M (Mem) 1087
MP (1414 or 1441) (Ant) 988; DP 1022
EP 701 (249); NP 1034
[OOR 1867, Rd 1924f & 2045f or 2048f; Pr 1088]

6. **Sun. FIFTH SUNDAY IN ORDINARY TIME 249**
MP 706; DP 994; EP 712; NP 1037
[OOR 1785, Rd 1924f & 2011f; TD Pr 249]

7. Mon. Monday of the 5th Week in Ordinary Time
MP 718; DP 998; EP 723; NP 1041
[OOR 1788, Rd 1924f & 2011f; Pr 249]

8. Tue. Weekday or St. Jerome Emiliani (1089) or St. Josephine Bakhita, V
(New) (1441)
MP (1473) (1441) (Ant) 728; DP 1003; EP (1473) (1444) (Ant) 734;
NP 1044
[OOR 1791, Rd 1924f & 2011f or 2049f or 2048f; Pr 1090 or 1443 or 249]

9. Wed. Wednesday of the 5th Week in Ordinary Time
MP 738; DP 1008; EP 743; NP 1046
[OOR 1794, Rd 1924f & 2011f; Pr 249]

10. Thu. St. Scholastica, V (Mem) 1090
MP (1441) (Ant) 748; DP 1012; EP (1444) (Ant) 754; NP 1049
[OOR 1797, Rd 1924f & 2048f; Pr 1091]

11. Fri. Weekday or Our Lady of Lourdes (1091)
MP (1372) (Ant) 759; DP 1017; EP (1378) (Ant) 765; NP 1052
[OOR 1800, Rd 1924f & 2011f or 1951f; Pr 1092 or 249]

12. Sat. Weekday or BVM on Saturday (1383)
     MP (1383) 770; DP 1022; EP (250) 775; NP 1034
     [OOR 1802, Rd 1924f & 2011f or 1951f; Pr 1386 or 249]

13. **Sun. SIXTH SUNDAY IN ORDINARY TIME 250**
     MP 780; DP 994; EP 786; NP 1037
     [OOR 1806, Rd 1924f & 2011f; TD Pr 250]

14. Mon. Sts. Cyril, Monk and Methodius, B (Mem) 1092
     MP (1426) (Ant) 792; DP 998; EP (1430) (Ant) 798; NP 1041
     [OOR 1809, Rd 1924f & 2046f; Pr 1093]

15. Tue. Tuesday of the 6th Week in Ordinary Time
     MP 802; DP 1003; EP 807; NP 1044
     [OOR 1812, Rd 1924f & 2011f; Pr 250]

16. Wed. Wednesday of the 6th Week in Ordinary Time
     MP 812; DP 1008; EP 818; NP 1046
     [OOR 1816, Rd 1924f & 2011f; Pr 250]

17. Thu. Weekday or Seven Founders of the Order of Servites (1093)
     MP (1470) (Ant) 824; DP 1012; EP (1471) (Ant) 830; NP 1049
     [OOR 1819, Rd 1924f & 2011f or 2049f; Pr 1093 or 250]

18. Fri. Friday of the 6th Week in Ordinary Time
     MP 835; DP 1017; EP 840; NP 1052
     [OOR 1821, Rd 1924f & 2011f; Pr 250]

19. Sat. Weekday or BVM on Saturday (1383)
     MP (1383) 845; DP 1022; EP (251) 851; NP 1034
     [OOR 1824, Rd 1924f & 2011f or 1951f; Pr 1386 or 250]

20. **Sun. SEVENTH SUNDAY IN ORDINARY TIME 251**
     MP 856; DP 994; EP 861; NP 1037
     [OOR 1827, Rd 1924f & 2011f; TD Pr 251]

21. Mon. Weekday or St. Peter Damian, B & D (1094)
     MP (1426 or 1435) (Ant) 867; DP 998
     EP (1430 or 1436) (Ant) 872; NP 1041
     [OOR 1829, Rd 1924f & 2011f or 2046f; Pr 1095 or 251]

22. Tue. CHAIR OF ST. PETER, AP (F) 1095
    MP 1095 (707); DP 1003; EP 1097 (1394); NP 1044
    [OOR 1831, Rd 1924f & 2043f; TD Pr 1097]

23. Wed. St. Polycarp, B & M (Mem) 1099
    MP (1414 or 1426) (Ant) 886; DP 1008
    EP (1417 or 1430) (Ant) 892; NP 1046
    [OOR 1835, Rd 1924f & 2045f or 2046f; Pr 1100]

24. Thu. Thursday of the 7th Week in Ordinary Time
    MP 897; DP 1012; EP 901; NP 1049
    [OOR 1838, Rd 1924f & 2011f; Pr 251]

25. Fri. Friday of the 7th Week in Ordinary Time
    MP 906; DP 1017; EP 911; NP 1052
    [OOR 1842, Rd 1924f & 2011f; Pr 251]

26. Sat. Weekday or BVM on Saturday (1383)
    MP (1383) 916; DP 1022; EP (252) 921; NP 1034
    [OOR 1845, Rd 1924f & 2011f or 1951f; Pr 1386 or 251]

27. **Sun. EIGHTH SUNDAY IN ORDINARY TIME 252**
    MP 925; DP 994; EP 931; NP 1037
    [OOR 1850, Rd 1924f & 2011f; TD Pr 252]

28. Mon. Monday of the 8th Week in Ordinary Time
    MP 937; DP 998; EP 942; NP 1041
    [OOR 1853, Rd 1924f & 2011f; Pr 252]

MARCH

1. Tue. Tuesday of the 8th Week in Ordinary Time
   MP 947; DP 1003; EP 953; NP 1044
   [OOR 1856, Rd 1924f & 2011f; Pr 252]

2. Wed. Ash Wednesday 255
   MP (255) 906 or 958; DP 1008; EP (256) 963; NP 1046
   [OOR 1859, Rd 1890f & 1968f; Pr 256]

3. Thu. Thursday after Ash Wednesday
   MP (258) 968 (St. Katharine Drexel, V [**New** (7) or 1443]); DP 1012
   EP (259) 973 (St. Katharine Drexel, V [(7) or 1443]); NP 1049
   [OOR 1861, Rd 1890f & 1968f; Pr (7) or 1443 or 259]

4.　Fri. Friday after Ash Wednesday
MP (261) 978 (St. Casimir 1101); DP 1017
EP (262) 984 (St. Casimir 1101); NP 1052
[OOR 1864, Rd 1890f & 1968f; Pr 1101 or 262]

5.　Sat. Saturday after Ash Wednesday
MP (264) 988; DP 1022; EP (266) 701; NP 1034
[OOR 1867, Rd 1890f & 1968f; Pr 265]

6.　**Sun. FIRST SUNDAY OF LENT 268**
MP (268) 707; DP 994; EP (270) 712; NP 1037
[OOR 1785, Rd 1890f & 1973f; Pr 269]

7.　Mon. Monday of the 1st Week of Lent
MP (272) 718 (Sts. Perpetua and Felicity, Mm 1102); DP 998
EP (273) 723 (Sts. Perpetua and Felicity, Mm 1102); NP 1041
[OOR 1788, Rd 1890f & 1968f; Pr 1102 or 273]

8.　Tue. Tuesday of the 1st Week of Lent
MP (275) 728 (St. John of God, Rel 1103); DP 1003
EP (276) 734 (St. John of God, Rel 1103); NP 1044
[OOR 1791, Rd 1890f & 1968f; Pr 1103 or 276]

9.　Wed. Wednesday of the 1st Week of Lent
MP (278) 738 (St. Frances of Rome, Rel 1104); DP 1008
EP (280) 743 (St. Frances of Rome, Rel 1104); NP 1046
[OOR 1794, Rd 1890f & 1968f; Pr 1104 or 279]

10.　Thu. Thursday of the 1st Week of Lent
MP (281) 748; DP 1012; EP (283) 754; NP 1049
[OOR 1797, Rd 1890f & 1968f; Pr 283]

11.　Fri. Friday of the 1st Week of Lent
MP (285) 759; DP 1017; EP (286) 765; NP 1052
[OOR 1800, Rd 1890f & 1968f; Pr 286]

12.　Sat. Saturday of the 1st Week of Lent
MP (288) 770; DP 1022; EP (290) 775; NP 1034
[OOR 1802, Rd 1890f & 1968f; Pr 289]

13.　**Sun. SECOND SUNDAY OF LENT 292**
MP (292) 780; DP 994; EP (294) 786; NP 1037
[OOR 1806, Rd 1890f & 1977f; Pr 293]

14. Mon. Monday of the 2nd Week of Lent
MP (296) 792; DP 998; EP (297) 798; NP 1041
[OOR 1809, Rd 1890f & 1968f; Pr 297]

15. Tue. Tuesday of the 2nd Week of Lent
MP (299) 802; DP 1003; EP (301) 807; NP 1044
[OOR 1812, Rd 1890f & 1968f; Pr 300]

16. Wed. Wednesday of the 2nd Week of Lent
MP (302) 812; DP 1008; EP (304) 818; NP 1046
[OOR 1816, Rd 1890f & 1968f; Pr 304]

17. Thu. Thursday of the 2nd Week of Lent
MP (306) 824 (St. Patrick, B 1105); DP 1012
EP (307) 830 (St. Patrick, B 1105); NP 1049
[OOR 1819, Rd 1890f & 1968f; Pr 1105 or 307]

18. Fri. Friday of the 2nd Week of Lent
MP (309) 835 (St. Cyril of Jerusalem, B & D 1106); DP 1017
EP 1107 (1448); NP 1034
[OOR 1821, Rd 1890f & 1968f; Pr 1106 or 310]

19. Sat. ST. JOSEPH, HUSBAND OF MARY (Sol) 1109
MP 1109 (707); DP 1027; EP 1111; NP 1037
[OOR 1824, Rd 1890f & 2055f; TD Pr 1110]

20. **Sun. THIRD SUNDAY OF LENT 316**
MP (316) 856; DP 994; EP (318) 861; NP 1037
[OOR 1827, Rd 1890f & 1968f; Pr 317]

21. Mon. Monday of the 3rd Week of Lent
MP (320) 867; DP 998; EP (322) 872; NP 1041
[OOR 1829, Rd 1890f & 1968f; Pr 321]

22. Tue. Tuesday of the 3rd Week of Lent
MP (323) 877; DP 1003; EP (324) 882; NP 1044
[OOR 1831, Rd 1890f & 1968f; Pr 324]

23. Wed. Wednesday of the 3rd Week of Lent
MP (326) 886 (St. Turibius de Mogrovejo, B 1113); DP 1008
EP (328) 892 (St. Turibius de Mogrovejo, B 1113); NP 1046
[OOR 1835, Rd 1890f & 1968f; Pr 1113 or 327]

24. Thu. Thursday of the 3rd Week of Lent
    MP (329) 897; DP 1012; EP 1114; NP 1034
    [OOR 1838, Rd 1890f & 1968f; Pr 1113 or 330]

25. Fri. ANNUNCIATION OF THE LORD (Sol) 1118
    MP 1118 (707); DP 1027; EP 1120; NP 1037
    [OOR 1842, Rd 1890f & 1956f; TD Pr 1119]

26. Sat. Saturday of the 3rd Week of Lent
    MP (335) 916; DP 1022; EP (338) 921; NP 1034
    [OOR 1845, Rd 1890f & 1968f; Pr 337]

27. **Sun. FOURTH SUNDAY OF LENT 340**
    MP (340) 925; DP 994; EP (342) 931; NP 1037
    [OOR 1850, Rd 1890f & 1968f; Pr 341]

28. Mon. Monday of the 4th Week of Lent
    MP (344) 937; DP 998; EP (346) 942; NP 1041
    [OOR 1853, Rd 1890f & 1968f; Pr 346]

29. Tue. Tuesday of the 4th Week of Lent
    MP (347) 947; DP 1003; EP (349) 953; NP 1044
    [OOR 1856, Rd 1890f & 1968f; Pr 349]

30. Wed. Wednesday of the 4th Week of Lent
    MP (351) 958; DP 1008; EP (352) 963; NP 1046
    [OOR 1859, Rd 1890f & 1968f; Pr 352]

31. Thu. Thursday of the 4th Week of Lent
    MP (354) 968; DP 1012; EP (355) 973; NP 1049
    [OOR 1861, Rd 1890f & 1968f; Pr 355]

APRIL

1. Fri. Friday of the 4th Week of Lent
    MP (357) 978; DP 1017; EP (358) 984; NP 1052
    [OOR 1864, Rd 1890f & 1968f; Pr 358]

2. Sat. Saturday of the 4th Week of Lent
    MP (360) 988 (St. Francis of Paola, Hermit 1124); DP 1022
    EP (362) 701; NP 1034
    [OOR 1867, Rd 1890f & 1968f; Pr 1124 or 361]

3. **Sun. FIFTH SUNDAY OF LENT 364**
   MP (364) 707; DP 994; EP (366) 712; NP 1037
   [OOR 1785, Rd 1890f & 1968f; Pr 365]

4. Mon. Monday of the 5th Week of Lent
   MP (368) 718 (St. Isidore, B & D 1125); DP 998
   EP (369) 723 (St. Isidore, B & D 1125); NP 1041
   [OOR 1788, Rd 1890f & 1968f; Pr 1125 or 369)

5. Tue. Tuesday of the 5th Week of Lent
   MP (371) 728 (St. Vincent Ferrer, P 1126); DP 1003
   EP (372) 734 (St. Vincent Ferrer, P 1126); NP 1044
   [OOR 1791, Rd 1890f & 1968f; Pr 1126 or 372]

6. Wed. Wednesday of the 5th Week of Lent
   MP (374) 738; DP 1008; EP (376) 743; NP 1046
   [OOR 1794, Rd 1890f & 1968f; Pr 375]

7. Thu. Thursday of the 5th Week of Lent
   MP (377) 748 (St. John Baptist de la Salle, P 1127); DP 1012
   EP (379) 754 (St. John Baptist de la Salle, P 1127); NP 1049
   [OOR 1797, Rd 1890f & 1968f; Pr 1127 or 378]

8. Fri. Friday of the 5th Week of Lent
   MP (380) 759; DP 1017; EP (382) 765; NP 1052
   [OOR 1800, Rd 1890f & 1968f; Pr 381]

9. Sat. Saturday of the 5th Week of Lent
   MP (383) 770; DP 1022; EP (386) 775; NP 1034
   [OOR 1802, Rd 1890f & 1968f; Pr 384]

10. **Sun. PASSION SUNDAY (PALM SUNDAY) 388**
    MP (388) 780; DP 994; EP (390) 786; NP 1037
    [OOR 1806, Rd 1890f & 1979f; Pr 390]

11. Mon. MONDAY OF HOLY WEEK
    MP (393) 792; DP 998; EP (395) 798; NP 1041
    [OOR 1809, Rd 1890f & 1981f; Pr 394]

12. Tue. TUESDAY OF HOLY WEEK
    MP (397) 802; DP 1003; EP (398) 807; NP 1044
    [OOR 1812, Rd 1890f & 1985f; Pr 398]

13. Wed. WEDNESDAY OF HOLY WEEK
    MP (400) 812; DP 1008; EP (402) 819; NP 1046
    [OOR 1816, Rd 1890f & 1981f or 1985f; Pr 402]

14. Thu. HOLY THURSDAY 404
    MP 824 (404); DP 1012; EP 830 (406); NP 1037
    [OOR 1819, Rd 1890f & 1982f; Pr 405]

15. Fri. GOOD FRIDAY 408
    MP 408; DP 1017; EP 413; NP 1037
    [OOR 1821, Rd 1890f & 1984f; Pr 413]

16. Sat. HOLY SATURDAY 417
    MP 417; DP 1022; EP 422; NP 1037
    [OOR 1824, Rd 1890f & 1987f; Pr 421]

17. **Sun. EASTER SUNDAY 427**
    MP 427 (707); DP 994; EP 429; NP 1037
    [OOR 1785, Rd 1910f & 1989f; TD Pr 428]

18. Mon. MONDAY WITHIN THE OCTAVE OF EASTER
    MP 427 & 434; DP 998; EP 429 & 435; NP 1034 or 1037
    [OOR 1788, Rd 1910f & 1989f; TD Pr 435]

19. Tue. TUESDAY WITHIN THE OCTAVE OF EASTER
    MP 427 & 437; DP 1003; EP 429 & 438; NP 1034 or 1037
    [OOR 1791, Rd 1910f & 1989f; TD Pr 438]

20. Wed. WEDNESDAY WITHIN THE OCTAVE OF EASTER
    MP 427 & 440; DP 1008; EP 429 & 441; NP 1034 or 1037
    [OOR 1794, Rd 1910f & 1989f; TD Pr 441]

21. Thu. THURSDAY WITHIN THE OCTAVE OF EASTER
    MP 427 & 443; DP 1012; EP 429 & 444; NP 1034 or 1037
    [OOR 1797, Rd 1910f & 1989f; TD Pr 444]

22. Fri. FRIDAY WITHIN THE OCTAVE OF EASTER
    MP 427 & 446; DP 1017; EP 429 & 447; NP 1034 or 1037
    [OOR 1800, Rd 1910f & 1989f; TD Pr 447]

23. Sat. SATURDAY WITHIN THE OCTAVE OF EASTER
    MP 427 & 449; DP 1022; EP 429 & 451; NP 1034 or 1037
    [OOR 1802, Rd 1910f & 1989f; TD Pr 450]

24. Sun. **SECOND SUNDAY OF EASTER 453**
    MP 427 & 453; DP 994; EP 429 & 455; NP 1037
    [OOR 1806, Rd 1910f & 1995f; TD Pr 454]

25. Mon. ST. MARK, EVANGELIST (F) 1132
    MP 1132 (707); DP 998; EP 1134 (1394); NP 1041
    [OOR 1809, Rd 1910f & 2043f; TD Pr 1134]

26. Tue. Tuesday of the 2nd Week of Easter
    MP (460) 802; DP 1003; EP (461) 807; NP 1044
    [OOR 1812, Rd 1910f & 1989f; Pr 461]

27. Wed. Wednesday of the 2nd Week of Easter
    MP (463) 812; DP 1008; EP (464) 818; NP 1046
    [OOR 1816, Rd 1910f & 1989f; Pr 464]

28. Thu. Easter Weekday or St. Peter Chanel, P & M (1136) or St. Louis
    Grignion de Montfort, P *(New)* (1426 or 1470)
    MP (1414) (1426 or 1470) (466) 824; DP 1012
    EP (1417) (1430 or 1471) (467) 830; NP 1049
    [OOR 1819, Rd 1910f & 1989f or 2045f or 2049f; Pr 1136 or *(New)*
    1429 or 1471 or 467]

29. Fri. St. Catherine of Siena, V & D (Mem) 1136
    MP (1441) (Ant) 835; DP 1017; EP (1444) (Ant) 840; NP 1052
    [OOR 1821, Rd 1910f & 2048f; Pr 1137]

30. Sat. Easter Weekday or St. Pius V, Po (1137)
    MP (1426) (471) 845; DP 1022; EP (1430) (474) 851; NP 1034
    [OOR 1824, Rd 1910f & 1989f or 2046f; Pr 1138 or 473]

MAY

1. Sun. **THIRD SUNDAY OF EASTER 476**
   MP (476) 856; DP 994; EP (478) 861; NP 1037
   [OOR 1827, Rd 1910f & 1989f; TD Pr 477]

2. Mon. St. Athanasius, B & D (Mem) 1142
   MP (1426 or 1435) 867; DP 998; EP (1430 or 1436) 872; NP 1041
   [OOR 1829, Rd 1910f & 2046f; Pr 1142)

3. Tue. STS. PHILIP AND JAMES, AP (F) 1143
   MP 1143 (707); DP 1003; EP 1145 (1394); NP 1044
   [OOR 1831, Rd 1910f & 2043f; TD Pr 1145]

4. Wed. Wednesday of the 3rd Week of Easter
    MP (486) 886; DP 1008; EP (487) 892; NP 1046
    [OOR 1835, Rd 1910f & 1989f; Pr 487]

5. Thu. Thursday of the 3rd Week of Easter
    MP (489) 897; DP 1012; EP (490) 901; NP 1049
    [OOR 1838, Rd 1910f & 1989f; Pr 490]

6. Fri. Friday of the 3rd Week of Easter
    MP (491) 906; DP 1017; EP (493) 911; NP 1052
    [OOR 1842, Rd 1910f & 1989f; Pr 492]

7. Sat. Saturday of the 3rd Week of Easter
    MP (494) 916; DP 1022; EP (496) 921; NP 1034
    [OOR 1845, Rd 1910f & 1989f; Pr 495]

8. **Sun. FOURTH SUNDAY OF EASTER 498**
    MP (498) 925; DP 994; EP (500) 931; NP 1037
    [OOR 1850, Rd 1910f & 1989f; TD Pr 499]

9. Mon. Monday of the 4th Week of Easter
    MP (502) 937; DP 998; EP (503) 942; NP 1041
    [OOR 1853, Rd 1910f & 1989f; Pr 503]

10. Tue. Easter Weekday or St. Damien de Veuster of Molokai, P *(New)* (1426)
    MP (1426) (505) 947; DP 1003; EP (1430) (506) 953; NP 1044
    [OOR 1856, Rd 1910f & 1989f or 2046f; Pr 1429 or 506]

11. Wed. Wednesday of the 4th Week of Easter
    MP (508) 958; DP 1008; EP (509) 963; NP 1046
    [OOR 1859, Rd 1910f & 1989f; Pr 509]

12. Thu. Easter Weekday or Sts. Nereus and Achilleus, Mm (1147) or St.
    Pancras, M (1148)
    MP (1402) (1414) (511) 968; DP 1012
    EP (1405) (1417) (512) 973; NP 1049
    [OOR 1861, Rd 1910f & 1989f or 2045f; Pr 1147 or 1148 or 512]

13. Fri. Easter Weekday or Our Lady of Fatima *(New)* Common of the
    Blessed Virgin Mary (1372)
    MP (1372) (514) 978; DP 1017; EP (1378) (515) 984; NP 1052
    [OOR 1864, Rd 1910f & 1989f or 1951f; Pr 1376 or 515]

14. Sat. ST. MATTHIAS, AP (F) 1148
    MP 1392 (Ant) (707); DP 1022; EP (519) 701; NP 1034
    [OOR 1867, Rd 1910f & 2043f; TD Pr 1149]

15. **Sun. FIFTH SUNDAY OF EASTER 521**
    MP (521) 707; DP 994; EP (523) 712; NP 1037
    [OOR 1785, Rd 1910f & 1989f; TD Pr 522]

16. Mon. Monday of the 5th Week of Easter
    MP (525) 718; DP 998; EP (526) 723; NP 1041
    [OOR 1788, Rd 1910f & 1989f; Pr 526]

17. Tue. Tuesday of the 5th Week of Easter
    MP (528) 728; DP 1003; EP (529) 734; NP 1044
    [OOR 1791, Rd 1910f & 1989f; Pr 529]

18. Wed. Easter Weekday or St. John I, Po & M (1150)
    MP (1414 or 1426) (531) 738; DP 1008
    EP (1417 or 1430) (532) 743; NP 1046
    [OOR 1794, Rd 1910f & 1989f or 2045f or 2046f; Pr 1150 or 532]

19. Thu. Thursday of the 5th Week of Easter
    MP (533) 748; DP 1012; EP (535) 754; NP 1049
    [OOR 1797, Rd 1910f & 1989f; Pr 534]

20. Fri. Easter Weekday or St. Bernardine of Siena, P (1150)
    MP (1426 or 1470) (536) 759; DP 1017
    EP (1430 or 1471) (538) 765; NP 1052
    [OOR 1800, Rd 1910f & 1989f or 2049f; Pr 1151 or 537]

21. Sat. Easter Weekday or St. Christopher Magallanes, P, and Comps, Mm
    (New) (1402 or 1426)
    MP (1402 or 1426) (539) 770; DP 1022; EP (541) 775; NP 1034
    [OOR 1802, Rd 1910f & 1989f or 2045f; Pr 1404 or 1429 or 540]

22. **Sun. SIXTH SUNDAY OF EASTER 543**
    MP (543) 781; DP 994; EP (545) 786; NP 1037
    [OOR 1806, Rd 1910f & 1989f; TD Pr 544]

23. Mon. Monday of the 6th Week of Easter
    MP (547) 792; DP 998; EP (548) 798; NP 1041
    [OOR 1809, Rd 1910f & 1989f; Pr 548]

24. Tue. Tuesday of the 6th Week of Easter
    MP (549) 802; DP 1003; EP (551) 807; NP 1044
    [OOR 1812, Rd 1910f & 1989f; Pr 551]

25. Wed. Easter Weekday or Venerable Bede, P & D (1151) or St. Gregory
    VII, Po (1152) or St. Mary Magdalene de Pazzi, V (1152)
    MP (1435 or 1470) (1426) (1441 or 1470) (552) 812; DP 1008
    EP 559; NP 1034

[OOR 1816, Rd 1910f & 1989f or 2046f or 2048f or 2049f; Pr 1151 or 1152 or 1153 or 554]

26. **Thu. ASCENSION (Sol) 562**
   MP (563) 707; DP 1027; EP 565; NP 1037
   [OOR 1819, Rd 1910f & 2005f; TD Pr 562]

27. Fri. Easter Weekday or St. Augustine of Canterbury, B (1154)
   MP (1426) (569) 835; DP 1017; EP (1430) (571) 840; NP 1052
   [OOR 1821, Rd 1910f & 1989f or 2046f; Pr 1154 or 571]

28. Sat. Saturday of the 6th Week of Easter
   MP (574) 845; DP 1022; EP (577) 851; NP 1034
   [OOR 1824, Rd 1910f & 1989f; Pr 576]

29. **Sun. SEVENTH SUNDAY OF EASTER 579**
   MP (579) 856; DP 994; EP (581) 861; NP 1037
   [OOR 1827, Rd 1910f & 1989f; TD Pr 580]

WHERE THE ASCENSION IS NOT TO BE OBSERVED AS A HOLYDAY OF OBLIGATION, IT IS ASSIGNED TO THE SEVENTH SUNDAY OF EASTER. **The specified rubrics below are to be followed until Monday of the 7th Week of Easter.**

25. Wed. Easter Weekday or Venerable Bede, P & D (1151) or St. Gregory VII, Po (1152) or St. Mary Magdalene de Pazzi, V (1152)
   MP (1435 or 1470) (1426) (1441 or 1470) (552) 812; DP 1008
   EP (1436 or 1471) (1430) (1444 or 1471) (554) 818; NP 1046
   [OOR 1816, Rd 1910f & 1989f or 2046f or 2048f or 2049f; Pr 1151 or 1152 or 1153 or 554]

26. Thu. St. Philip Neri, P (Mem) 1153
   MP (1426 or 1470) 824; DP 1012; EP (1430 or 1471) 830; NP 1049
   [OOR 1819, Rd 1910f & 2046f or 2049f; Pr 1153]

27. Fri. Easter Weekday or St. Augustine of Canterbury, B (1154)
   MP (1426) (569) 835; DP 1017; EP (1430) (571) 840; NP 1052
   [OOR 1821, Rd 1910f & 1989f or 2046f; Pr 1154 or 570]

28. Sat. Saturday of the 6th Week of Easter
   MP (574) 845; DP 1022; EP 559; NP 1034
   [OOR 1824, Rd 1910f & 1989f; Pr 575]

29. **Sun. ASCENSION (Sol) 562**
   MP (563) 707; DP 1027; EP 565; NP 1037
   [OOR 1827, Rd 1910f & 2005f; TD Pr 562]

30. Mon. Monday of the 7th Week of Easter
    MP (583) 867; DP 998; EP (584) 872; NP 1041
    [OOR 1829, Rd 1910f & 1989f; Pr 584]

31. Tue. VISITATION (F) 1154
    MP 1154 (707); DP 1003; EP 1156 (1378); NP 1044
    [OOR 1831, Rd 1910f & 1953f; TD Pr 1156]

JUNE

1. Wed. St. Justin, M (Mem) 1160
   MP (1414) (Ant) 886; DP 1008
   EP (1417) (Ant) 892; NP 1046
   [OOR 1835, Rd 1910f & 2045f; Pr 1160]

2. Thu. Easter Weekday or Sts. Marcellinus and Peter, Mm (1161)
   MP (1402) (591) 897; DP 1012; EP (1405) (592) 901; NP 1049
   [OOR 1838, Rd 1910f & 1989f or 2045f; Pr 1161 or 592]

3. Fri. St. Charles Lwanga and Comps, Mm (Mem) 1161
   MP (1402) 906; DP 1017; EP (1405) 911; NP 1052
   [OOR 1842, Rd 1910f & 2045f; Pr 1162]

4. Sat. Saturday of the 7th Week of Easter
   MP (597) 916; DP 1022; EP 599; NP 1034
   [OOR 1845, Rd 1910f & 1989f; Pr 598]

5. **Sun. PENTECOST (Sol) 603**
   MP 603 (707); DP 1027; EP 605; NP 1037
   [OOR 1850, Rd 1910f & 2008f; TD Pr 605]

6. Mon. The Blessed Virgin Mary, Mother of the Church (Mem) *(New)*
         Common of the Blessed Virgin Mary (1372)
   MP (1372) 792; DP 998; EP (1378) 798; NP 1041
   [OOR 1809, Rd 1924f & 1951f; Pr 39 in this Guide]

7. Tue. Tuesday of the 10th Week in Ordinary Time
   MP 802; DP 1003; EP 807; NP 1044
   [OOR 1812, Rd 1924f & 2011f; Pr 614]

8. Wed. Wednesday of the 10th Week in Ordinary Time
   MP 812; DP 1008; EP 818; NP 1046
   [OOR 1816, Rd 1924f & 2011f; Pr 614]

9.   Thu. Weekday or St. Ephrem, De & D (1164)
     MP (1435) 824; DP 1012; EP (1436) 830; NP 1049
     [OOR 1819, Rd 1924f & 2011f or 2053f; Pr 1164 or 614]

10. Fri. Friday of the 10th Week in Ordinary Time
     MP 835; DP 1017; EP 840; NP 1052
     [OOR 1821, Rd 1924f & 2011f; Pr 614]

11. Sat. St. Barnabas, Ap (Mem) 1164
     MP (1165) 845; DP 1022; EP 641; NP 1034
     [OOR 1824, Rd 1924f & 2043f; Pr 1166]

12. **Sun. TRINITY SUNDAY (Sol) 645**
     MP 645 (707); DP 1027; EP 648; NP 1037
     [OOR 1827, Rd 1924f & 2003f or 2009f; TD Pr 645]

13. Mon. St. Anthony of Padua, P & D (Mem) 1168
     MP (1426 or 1435 or 1470) 867; DP 998
     EP (1430 or 1436 or 1471) 872; NP 1041
     [OOR 1829, Rd 1924f & 2046f; Pr 1168]

14. Tue. Tuesday of the 11th Week in Ordinary Time
     MP 877; DP 1003; EP 882; NP 1044
     [OOR 1831, Rd 1924f & 2011f; Pr 615]

15. Wed. Wednesday of the 11th Week in Ordinary Time
     MP 886; DP 1008; EP 892; NP 1046
     [OOR 1835, Rd 1924f & 2011f; Pr 615]

16. Thu. Thursday of the 11th Week in Ordinary Time
     MP 897; DP 1012; EP 901; NP 1049
     [OOR 1838, Rd 1924f & 2011f; Pr 615]

17. Fri. Friday of the 11th Week in Ordinary Time
     MP 906; DP 1017; EP 911; NP 1052
     [OOR 1842, Rd 1924f & 2011f; Pr 615]

18. Sat. Weekday or BVM on Saturday (1383)
     MP (1383) 916; DP 1022; EP 652; NP 1034
     [OOR 1845, Rd 1924f & 2011f or 1951f; Pr 1386 or 615]

19. **Sun. CORPUS CHRISTI (Sol) 656**
     MP 656 (707); DP 1027; EP 658; NP 1037
     [OOR 1850, Rd 1924f & 2002f or 2011f; TD Pr 656]

20. Mon. Monday of the 12th Week in Ordinary Time
    MP 937; DP 998; EP 942; NP 1041
    [OOR 1853, Rd 1924f & 2011f; Pr 616]

21. Tue. St. Aloysius Gonzaga, Rel (Mem) 1169
    MP (1470) 947; DP 1003; EP (1471) 953; NP 1044
    [OOR 1856, Rd 1924f & 2049f; Pr 1170]

22. Wed. Weekday or St. Paulinus of Nola, B (1170) or Sts. John Fisher,
    B & M and Thomas More, M (1171)
    MP (1426) (1402) 958; DP 1008; EP 1172 (1448); NP 1034
    [OOR 1859, Rd 1924f & 2011f or 2045f or 2046f; Pr 1170 or 1171 or 616]

23. Thu. BIRTH OF ST. JOHN THE BAPTIST (Sol) 1174
    MP 1174 (707); DP 1027; EP 663; NP 1034
    [OOR 1861, Rd 1924f & 1948f; TD Pr 1173]

24. Fri. SACRED HEART (Sol) 667
    MP 667 (707); DP 1027; EP 669; NP 1037
    [OOR 1864, Rd 1924f & 2012f; TD Pr 666]

25. Sat. Immaculate Heart of Mary (Mem) (1159)
    MP (1372) (Ant) 988; DP 1022; EP 701 (617); NP 1034
    [OOR 1867, Rd 1924f & 1951f; Pr 1159]

26. **Sun. THIRTEENTH SUNDAY IN ORDINARY TIME 617**
    MP 706; DP 994; EP 712; NP 1037
    [OOR 1785, Rd 1924f & 2011f; TD Pr 617]

27. Mon. Weekday or St. Cyril of Alexandria, B & D (1178)
    MP (1426 or 1435) 718; DP 998; EP (1430 or 1436) 723; NP 1041
    [OOR 1788, Rd 1924f & 2011f or 2046f; Pr 1178 or 617]

28. Tue. St. Irenaeus, B & M (Mem) 1178
    MP (1414 or 1426) (Ant) 728; DP 1003; EP 1179 (1389); NP 1034
    [OOR 1791, Rd 1924f & 2045f; Pr 1179]

29. Wed. STS. PETER AND PAUL, AP (Sol) 1181
    MP 1181 (707); DP 1027; EP 1183 (1394); NP 1037
    [OOR 1794, Rd 1924f & 2043f; TD Pr 1183]

30. Thu. Weekday or First Martyrs of the Church of Rome (1185)
    MP (1402) (Ant) 748; DP 1012; EP (1405) (Ant) 754; NP 1049
    [OOR 1797, Rd 1924f & 2011f or 2045f; Pr 1186 or 617]

JULY

1. Fri. Weekday or St. Junipero Serra, P **(New)** (8)
    MP (1426 or 1470) 759; Pr (8) or 1429; DP 1017
    EP (1430 or 1471) 765; Pr (8) or 1429; NP 1052
    [OOR 1800, Rd 1924f & 2011f or 2046f; Pr (8) or 1429 or 617]

2. Sat. Weekday or BVM on Saturday (1383)
    MP (1383) 770; DP 1022; EP (618) 775; NP 1034
    [OOR 1802, Rd 1924f & 2011f or 1951f; Pr 1386 or 617]

3. Sun. **FOURTEENTH SUNDAY IN ORDINARY TIME 618**
    MP 780; DP 994; EP 786; NP 1037
    [OOR 1806, Rd 1924f & 2011f; TD Pr 618]

4. Mon. Monday of the 14th Week in Ordinary Time
    MP 792; DP 998; EP 798; NP 1041
    [OOR 1809, Rd 1924f & 2011f; Pr 618]

5. Tue. Weekday or St. Anthony Zaccaria, P (1190) or St. Elizabeth of
    Portugal (1189) **[transferred from 7/4]**
    MP (1426 or 1473 or 1470) (1472) 802; DP 1003
    EP (1430 or 1473 or 1471) (1472) 807; NP 1044
    [OOR 1812, Rd 1924f & 2011f or 2046f or 2053f; Pr 1190 or 1189 or 618]

6. Wed. Weekday or St. Maria Goretti, V & M (1190)
    MP (1414 or 1441) 812; DP 1008; EP (1417 or 1444) 818; NP 1046
    [OOR 1816, Rd 1924f & 2011f or 2045f; Pr 1190 or 618]

7. Thu. Thursday of the 14th Week in Ordinary Time
    MP 824; DP 1012; EP 830; NP 1049
    [OOR 1819, Rd 1924f & 2011f; Pr 618]

8. Fri. Friday of the 14th Week in Ordinary Time
    MP 835; DP 1017; EP 840; NP 1052
    [OOR 1821, Rd 1924f & 2011f; Pr 618]

9. Sat. Weekday or St. Augustine Zhao Rong, P, and Comps, Mm *(New)*
    (1402 or 1426) or BVM on Saturday (1383)
    MP (1402 or 1426) (1383) 845; DP 1022; EP (619) 851; NP 1034
    [OOR 1824, Rd 1924f & 2011f or 2045f or 1951f; Pr 1404 or 1429 or
    1386 or 618]

10. Sun. **FIFTEENTH SUNDAY IN ORDINARY TIME 619**
    MP 856; DP 994; EP 861; NP 1037
    [OOR 1827, Rd 1924f & 2011f; TD Pr 619]

11. Mon. St. Benedict, Ab (Mem) 1191
    MP (1470) (Ant) 867; DP 998; EP (1471) (Ant) 872; NP 1041
    [OOR 1829, Rd 1924f & 2049f; Pr 1191]

12. Tue. Tuesday of the 15th Week in Ordinary Time
    MP 877; DP 1003; EP 882; NP 1044
    [OOR 1831, Rd 1924f & 2011f; Pr 619]

13. Wed. Weekday or St. Henry (1192)
    MP (1452) 886; DP 1008; EP (1455) 892; NP 1046
    [OOR 1835, Rd 1924f & 2011f or 2053f; Pr 1192 or 619]

14. Thu. St. Kateri Tekakwitha, V (Mem) **(New)** (9)
    MP (1441) 897; Pr proper (9) or 1443; DP 1012
    EP (1444) 901; Pr proper (9) or 1443; NP 1049
    [OOR 1838, Rd 1924f & 2048f; Pr proper (9) or 1443]

15. Fri. St. Bonaventure, B & D (Mem) 1193
    MP (1426 or 1435) 906; DP 1017; EP (1430 or 1436) 911; NP 1052
    [OOR 1842, Rd 1924f & 2046f; Pr 1194]

16. Sat. Weekday or Our Lady of Mount Carmel (1194) or BVM on Saturday
    (1383)
    MP (1372) (1383) (Ant) 916; DP 1022; EP (620) 921; NP 1034
    [OOR 1845, Rd 1924f & 2011f or 1951f; Pr 1194 or 1386 or 619]

17. **Sun. SIXTEENTH SUNDAY IN ORDINARY TIME 620**
    MP 925; DP 994; EP 931; NP 1037
    [OOR 1850, Rd 1924f & 2011f; TD Pr 620]

18. Mon. Weekday or St. Camillus de Lellis, P (1193) **[transferred from 7/14]**
    MP (1472) 937; DP 998; EP (1472) 942; NP 1041
    [OOR 1853, Rd 1924f & 2011f or 2046f; Pr 1193 or 620]

19. Tue. Tuesday of the 16th Week in Ordinary Time
    MP 947; DP 1003; EP 953; NP 1044
    [OOR 1856, Rd 1924f & 2011f; Pr 620]

20. Wed. Weekday or St. Apollinaris, B & M *(New)* (1414 or 1426)
    MP (1414 or 1426) 958; DP 1008
    EP (1417 or 1430) 963; NP 1046
    [OOR 1859, Rd 1924f & 2011f or 2045f or 2046f; Pr 1416 or 1428 or 620]

21. Thu. Weekday or St. Lawrence of Brindisi, P & D (1195)
    MP (1426 or 1435) 968; DP 1012

EP (1430 or 1436) 973; NP 1049
[OOR 1861, Rd 1924f & 2011f or 2046f; Pr 1195 or 620]

22. Fri. ST. MARY MAGDALENE (F) 1195
MP 1196 (707); DP 1017; EP 1197 (1466); NP 1049
[OOR 1864, Rd 1924f & 2053f; TD Pr 1197]

23. Sat. Weekday or St. Bridget, Rel (1198) or BVM on Saturday (1383)
MP (1470) (1383) 988; DP 1022; EP (621) 701; NP 1034
[OOR 1867, Rd 1924f & 2011f or 2049f or 1951f; Pr 1198 or 1386 or 620]

24. **Sun. SEVENTEENTH SUNDAY IN ORDINARY TIME 621**
MP 706; DP 994; EP 712; NP 1037
[OOR 1785, Rd 1924f & 2011f; TD Pr 621]

25. Mon. ST. JAMES, AP (F) 1199
MP 1199 (707); DP 998; EP 1200 (1394); NP 1041
[OOR 1788, Rd 1924f & 2043f; TD Pr 1200]

26. Tue. Sts. Joachim and Ann, Parents of Mary (Mem) 1201
MP 1202 (728); DP 1003; EP 1203 (734); NP 1044
[OOR 1791, Rd 1924f & 2053f; Pr 1202]

27. Wed. Wednesday of the 17th Week in Ordinary Time
MP 738; DP 1008; EP 743; NP 1046
[OOR 1794, Rd 1924f & 2011f; Pr 621]

28. Thu. Thursday of the 17th Week in Ordinary Time
MP 748; DP 1012; EP 754; NP 1049
[OOR 1797, Rd 1924f & 2011f; Pr 621]

29. Fri. St. Martha (Mem) 1203
MP (1463) (Ant) 759; DP 1017; EP (1466) (Ant) 765; NP 1052
[OOR 1800, Rd 1924f & 2053f; Pr 1204]

30. Sat. Weekday or St. Peter Chrysologus, B & D (1204) or BVM on Saturday (1383)
MP (1426 or 1435) (1383) 770; DP 1022; EP (622) 775; NP 1034
[OOR 1802, Rd 1924f & 2011f or 2046f or 1951f; Pr 1205 or 1386 or 621]

31. **Sun. EIGHTEENTH SUNDAY IN ORDINARY TIME 622**
MP 780; DP 994; EP 786; NP 1037
[OOR 1806, Rd 1924f & 2011f; TD Pr 622]

AUGUST

1. Mon. St. Alphonsus Liguori, B & D (Mem) 1206
   MP (1426 or 1435) 792; DP 998
   EP (1430 or 1436) 798; NP 1041
   [OOR 1809, Rd 1924f & 2046f; Pr 1207]

2. Tue. Weekday or St. Eusebius of Vercelli, B (1207) or St. Peter Julian
      Eymard, P *(New)* (1426 or 1470)
   MP (1426) (1470) 802; DP 1003
   EP (1430) (1471) 807; NP 1044
   [OOR 1812, Rd 1924f & 2011f or 2046f; Pr 1207 or 1429 or 1471 or 622]

3. Wed. Wednesday of the 18th Week in Ordinary Time
   MP 812; DP 1008; EP 818; NP 1046
   [OOR 1816, Rd 1924f & 2011f; Pr 622]

4. Thu. St. John Vianney, P (Mem) 1208
   MP (1426) 824; DP 1012; EP (1430) 830; NP 1049
   [OOR 1819, Rd 1924f & 2046f; Pr 1208]

5. Fri. Weekday or Dedication of St. Mary Major (1208)
   MP (1372) (Ant) 835; DP 1017; EP (1378) 840; NP 1052
   [OOR 1821, Rd 1924f & 2011f or 1951f; Pr 1209 or 622]

6. Sat. TRANSFIGURATION (F) 1213
   MP 1213 (707); DP 1022; EP 851 (623); NP 1034
   [OOR 1824, Rd 1924f & 1977f; TD Pr 1215]

7. **Sun. NINETEENTH SUNDAY IN ORDINARY TIME 623**
   MP 856; DP 994; EP 861; NP 1037
   [OOR 1827, Rd 1924f & 2011f; TD Pr 624]

8. Mon. St. Dominic, P (Mem) 1220
   MP (1426 or 1470) 867; DP 998; EP (1430 or 1471) 872; NP 1041
   [OOR 1829, Rd 1924f & 2046f or 2049f; Pr 1221]

9. Tue. Weekday or St. Teresa Benedicta of the Cross, V & M (Edith Stein)
      (New) (1414 or 1441)
   MP (1414 or 1441) 877; DP 1003; EP (1417 or 1444) 882; NP 1044
   [OOR 1831, Rd 1924f & 2011f or 2045f or 2048f; Pr 1417 or 1443 or 624]

10. Wed. ST. LAWRENCE, DE & M (F) 1221
    MP 1221 (707); DP 1008; EP 1223 (1414); NP 1046
    [OOR 1835, Rd 1924f & 2045f; TD Pr 1222]

11. Thu. St. Clare, V (Mem) 1224
    MP (1441 or 1470) 897; DP 1012; EP (1444 or 1471) 901; NP 1049
    [OOR 1838, Rd 1924f & 2048f; Pr 1224

12. Fri. Weekday or St. Jane Frances de Chantal, Rel (1340) or **(New)** (14)
    [transferred from 8/18]
    MP (1470) 906; DP 1017; EP (1471) 911; NP 1052
    [OOR 1842, Rd 1924f & 2011f or 2016f; Pr 1340 or (17) or 624]

13. Sat. Weekday or Sts. Pontian, Po & M and Hippolytus, P & M (1224) or
    BVM on Saturday (1383)
    MP (1402 or 1426) (1383) 916; DP 1022; EP (624) 921; NP 1034
    [OOR 1845, Rd 1924f & 2011f or 2045f or 1951f; Pr 1225 or 1386 or 624]

14. **Sun. TWENTIETH SUNDAY IN ORDINARY TIME 624**
    MP 925; DP 994; EP 1225 (1368); NP 1034
    [OOR 1850, Rd 1924f & 2011f; TD Pr 625]

15. **Mon. ASSUMPTION (Sol) 1227**
    MP 1227 (707); DP 1027; EP 1229 (1378); NP 1037
    [OOR 1853, Rd 1924f & 1951f; TD Pr 1229]

16. Tue. Weekday or St. Stephen of Hungary (1231)
    MP (1452) 947; DP 1003; EP (1455) 953; NP 1044
    [OOR 1856, Rd 1924f & 2011f or 2053f; Pr 1231 or 625]

17. Wed. Wednesday of the 20th Week in Ordinary Time
    MP 958; DP 1008; EP 963; NP 1046
    [OOR 1859, Rd 1924f & 2011f; Pr 625]

18. Thu. Thursday of the 20th Week in Ordinary Time
    MP 968; DP 1012; EP 973; NP 1049
    [OOR 1861, Rd 1924f & 2011f; Pr 625]

19. Fri. Weekday or St. John Eudes, P (1232)
    MP (1426 or 1470) 978; DP 1017; EP (1430 or 1471) 984; NP 1052
    [OOR 1864, Rd 1924f & 2011f or 2046f; Pr 1232 or 625]

20. Sat. St. Bernard, Ab & D (Mem) 1232
    MP (1435 or 1470) (Ant) 988; DP 1022; EP 701 (626); NP 1034
    [OOR 1867, Rd 1924f & 2049f; Pr 1233]

21. **Sun. TWENTY-FIRST SUNDAY IN ORDINARY TIME 626**
    MP 706; DP 994; EP 712; NP 1037
    [OOR 1785, Rd 1924f & 2011f; TD Pr 626]

22. Mon. Queenship of Mary (Mem) 1234
MP (1372) (Ant) 718; DP 998; EP (1378) (Ant) 723; NP 1041
[OOR 1788, Rd 1924f & 1951f; Pr 1234]

23. Tue. Weekday or St. Rose of Lima, V (1235)
MP (1441 or 1470) 728; DP 1003; EP (1444 or 1471) 734; NP 1044
[OOR 1791, Rd 1924f & 2011f or 2048f; Pr 1235 or 626]

24. Wed. ST. BARTHOLOMEW, AP (F) 1236
MP 1392 (707); DP 1008; EP 1394; NP 1046
[OOR 1794, Rd 1924f & 2043f; TD Pr 1236]

25. Thu. Weekday or St. Louis (1236) or St. Joseph Calasanz, P (1237)
MP (1452) (1473 or 1426) 748; DP 1012
EP (1455) (1473 or 1430) 754; NP 1049
[OOR 1797, Rd 1924f & 2011f or 2053f; Pr 1236 or 1237 or 626]

26. Fri. Friday of the 21st Week in Ordinary Time
MP 759; DP 1017; EP 765; NP 1052
[OOR 1800, Rd 1924f & 2011f; Pr 626]

27. Sat. St. Monica (Mem) 1238
MP (1463) (Ant) 770; DP 1022; EP 775 (627); NP 1034
[OOR 1802, Rd 1924f & 2053f; Pr 1238]

28. **Sun. TWENTY-SECOND SUNDAY IN ORDINARY TIME 627**
MP 780; DP 994; EP 786; NP 1037
[OOR 1806, Rd 1924f & 2011f; TD Pr 627]

29. Mon. Beheading of St. John the Baptist, M (Mem) 1240
MP 1240 (707); DP 998; EP 1242 (1417); NP 1041
[OOR 1809, Rd 1924f & 2045f; Pr 1241]

30. Tue. Tuesday of the 22nd Week in Ordinary Time
MP 802; DP 1003; EP 807; NP 1044
[OOR 1812, Rd 1924f & 2011f; Pr 627]

31. Wed. Wednesday of the 22nd Week in Ordinary Time
MP 812; DP 1008; EP 818; NP 1046
[OOR 1816, Rd 1924f & 2011f; Pr 627]

SEPTEMBER

1. Thu. Thursday of the 22nd Week in Ordinary Time
MP 824; DP 1012; EP 830; NP 1049
[OOR 1819, Rd 1924f & 2011f; Pr 627]

2.   Fri. Friday of the 22nd Week in Ordinary Time
      MP 835; DP 1017; EP 840; NP 1052
      [OOR 1821, Rd 1924f & 2011f; Pr 627]

3.   Sat. St. Gregory the Great, Po & D (Mem) 1244
      MP (1426 or 1435) (Ant) 845; DP 1022; EP (628) 851; NP 1034
      [OOR 1824, Rd 1924f & 2046f; Pr 1244]

4.   **Sun. TWENTY-THIRD SUNDAY IN ORDINARY TIME 628**
      MP 856; DP 994; EP 861; NP 1037
      [OOR 1827, Rd 1924f & 2011f; TD Pr 628]

5.   Mon. Monday of the 23rd Week in Ordinary Time
      MP 867; DP 998; EP 872; NP 1041
      [OOR 1829, Rd 1924f & 2011f; Pr 628]

6.   Tue. Tuesday of the 23rd Week in Ordinary Time
      MP 877; DP 1003; EP 882; NP 1044
      [OOR 1831, Rd 1924f & 2011f; Pr 628]

7.   Wed. Wednesday of the 23rd Week in Ordinary Time
      MP 886; DP 1008; EP 892; NP 1046
      [OOR 1835, Rd 1924f & 2011f; Pr 628]

8.   Thu. BIRTH OF MARY (F) 1245
      MP 1245 (707); DP 1012; EP 1247 (1378); NP 1049
      [OOR 1838, Rd 1924f & 1951f; TD Pr 1246]

9.   Fri. St. Peter Claver, P (Mem) 1248
      MP (1426 or 1472) 906; DP 1017; EP (1430 or 1472) 911; NP 1052
      [OOR 1842, Rd 1924f & 2046f; Pr 1249]

10. Sat. Weekday or BVM on Saturday (1383)
      MP (1383) 916; DP 1022; EP (629) 921; NP 1034
      [OOR 1845, Rd 1924f & 2011f or 1951f; Pr 1386 or 628]

11. **Sun. TWENTY-FOURTH SUNDAY IN ORDINARY TIME 629**
      MP 925; DP 994; EP 931; NP 1037
      [OOR 1850, Rd 1924f & 2011f; TD Pr 629]

12. Mon. Weekday or The Most Holy Name of Mary *(New)* Common of the
         Blessed Virgin Mary (1372)
      MP (1372) (Ant) 937; DP 998; EP (1378) 942; NP 1041
      [OOR 1853, Rd 1924f & 2011f or 1951f; Pr 1376f or 629]

13. Tue. St. John Chrysostom, B & D (Mem) 1249
      MP (1426 or 1435) 947; DP 1003

EP (1430 or 1436) 953; NP 1044
[OOR 1856, Rd 1924f & 2046f; Pr 1250]

14. Wed. TRIUMPH OF THE CROSS (F) 1254
MP 1254 (707); DP 1008; EP 1256; NP 1046
[OOR 1859, Rd 1924f & 1984f; TD Pr 1256]

15. Thu. Our Lady of Sorrows (Mem) 1260
MP 1261 (707); DP 1012; EP 1262 (1378); NP 1049
[OOR 1861, Rd 1924f & 1951f; Pr 1262]

16. Fri. Sts. Cornelius, Po & M and Cyprian, B & M (Mem) 1263
MP (1402 or 1426) (Ant) 978; DP 1017
EP (1405 or 1430) (Ant) 984; NP 1052
[OOR 1864, Rd 1924f & 2045f; Pr 1264]

17. Sat. Weekday or St. Robert Bellarmine, B & D (1265) or BVM on
Saturday (1383)
MP (1426 or 1435) (1383) 988; DP 1022; EP (630) 701; NP 1034
[OOR 1867, Rd 1924f & 2011f or 2046f or 1951f; Pr 1265 or 1386 or 629]

18. **Sun. TWENTY-FIFTH SUNDAY IN ORDINARY TIME 630**
MP 706; DP 994; EP 712; NP 1037
[OOR 1785, Rd 1924f & 2011f; TD Pr 631]

19. Mon. Weekday or St. Januarius, B & M (1265)
MP (1414 or 1426) 718; DP 998; EP (1417 or 1430) 723; NP 1041
[OOR 1788, Rd 1924f & 2011f or 2045f; Pr 1266 or 631]

20. Tue. Sts. Andrew Kim Taegŏn, P & M, Paul Chŏng Hasang, and Comps,
Mm (Mem) **(New)** (17)
MP (1402) 728; Pr proper (21); DP 1003; EP (1405) 734; NP 1044
[OOR 1791, Rd 1924f & 2045f & proper (18); Pr proper (21) or 1404]

21. Wed. ST. MATTHEW, AP & EVANGELIST (F) 1266
MP 1392 (707) (Ant); DP 1008; EP 1394 (Ant); NP 1046
[OOR 1794, Rd 1924f & 2043f; TD Pr 1266]

22. Thu. Thursday of the 25th Week in Ordinary Time
MP 748; DP 1012; EP 754; NP 1049
[OOR 1797, Rd 1924f & 2011f; Pr 631]

23. Fri. St. Pius of Pietrelcina, P (Mem) *(New)* (1426)
MP (1426) 759; DP 1017; EP (1430) 765; NP 1052
[OOR 1800, Rd 1924f & 2046f; Pr 1429]

24.   Sat. Weekday or BVM on Saturday (1383)
      MP (1383) 770; DP 1022; EP (631) 775; NP 1034
      [OOR 1802, Rd 1924f & 2011f or 1951f; Pr 1386 or 631]

25.   **Sun. TWENTY-SIXTH SUNDAY IN ORDINARY TIME 632**
      MP 780; DP 994; EP 786; NP 1037
      [OOR 1806, Rd 1924f & 2011f; TD Pr 632]

26.   Mon. Weekday or Sts. Cosmas and Damian, Mm (1267)
      MP (1402) 792; DP 998; EP (1405) 798; NP 1041
      [OOR 1809, Rd 1924f & 2011f or 2045f; Pr 1267 or 632]

27.   Tue. St. Vincent de Paul, P (Mem) 1267
      MP (1426 or 1472) (Ant) 802; DP 1003
      EP (1430 or 1472) (Ant) 807; NP 1044
      [OOR 1812, Rd 1924f & 2046f; Pr 1268]

28.   Wed. Weekday or St. Wenceslaus, M (1268) or St. Lawrence Ruiz and
          Comps, Mm **(New)** (21); Pr proper (24) or 1404
      MP (1414) (1402) 812; DP 1008; EP (1417) (1405) 818; NP 1046
      [OOR 1816, Rd 1924f & 2011f or 2045f or proper (22); Pr 1269 or
          proper (24) or 1404 or 632]

29.   Thu. STS. MICHAEL, GABRIEL AND RAPHAEL, ARCHANGELS (F) 1269
      MP 1269 (707); DP 1012; EP 1271; NP 1049
      [OOR 1819, Rd 1924f & 2011f; TD Pr 1271]

30.   Fri. St. Jerome, P & D (Mem) 1275
      MP (1435) 835; DP 1017; EP (1436) 840; NP 1052
      [OOR 1821, Rd 1924f & 2046f; Pr 1275]

OCTOBER

1.   Sat. St. Theresa of the Child Jesus, V & D (Mem) 1276
      MP (1441 or 1435) (Ant) 845; DP 1022
      EP 851 (633); NP 1034
      [OOR 1824, Rd 1924f & 2048f; Pr 1276]

2.   **Sun. TWENTY-SEVENTH SUNDAY IN ORDINARY TIME 633**
      MP 856; DP 994; EP 861; NP 1037
      [OOR 1827, Rd 1924f & 2011f; TD Pr 633]

3.   Mon. Monday of the 27th Week in Ordinary Time
      MP 867; DP 998; EP 872; NP 1041
      [OOR 1829, Rd 1924f & 2011f; Pr 633]

4. Tue. St. Francis of Assisi (Mem) 1283
   MP (1470) (Ant) 877; DP 1003; EP (1471) (Ant) 882; NP 1044
   [OOR 1831, Rd 1924f & 2049f; Pr 1283]

5. Wed. Weekday or St. Faustina Kowalska, V *(New)* (1441 or 1470) or Bl.
   Francis Xavier Seelos, P *(New)* (1426)
   MP (1441 or 1470) (1426) 886; DP 1008
   EP (1444 or 1471) (1430) 892; NP 1046
   [OOR 1835, Rd 1924f & 2011f or 2048f or 2046f; Pr 1443 or 1471 or
   1429 or 633]

6. Thu. Weekday or St. Bruno, P (1284) or Bl. Marie Rose Durocher, V
   (New) Pr proper (25)
   MP (1426 or 1470) (1441) 897; DP 1012
   EP (1430 or 1471) (1444) 901; NP 1049
   [OOR 1838, Rd 1924f & 2011f or 2046f or 2048f; Pr 1284 or proper
   (25) or 1443 or 633]

7. Fri. Our Lady of the Rosary (Mem) 1284
   MP 1285 (707); DP 1017; EP 1286 (1378); NP 1052
   [OOR 1842, Rd 1924f & 1951f; Pr 1286]

8. Sat. Weekday or BVM on Saturday (1383)
   MP (1383) 916; DP 1022; EP (634) 921; NP 1034
   [OOR 1845, Rd 1924f & 2011f or 1951f; Pr 1386 or 633)

9. **Sun. TWENTY-EIGHTH SUNDAY IN ORDINARY TIME 634**
   MP 925; DP 994; EP 931; NP 1037
   [OOR 1850, Rd 1924f & 2011f; TD Pr 634]

10. Mon. Monday of the 28th Week in Ordinary Time
    MP 937; DP 998; EP 942; NP 1041
    [OOR 1853, Rd 1924f & 2011f; Pr 634]

11. Tue. Weekday or St. John XXIII, Po *(New)* (1426)
    MP (1426) 947; DP 1003; (1430) 953; NP 1044
    [OOR 1856, Rd 1924f & 2011f or 2046f; Pr 1428 or 634]

12. Wed. Wednesday of the 28th Week in Ordinary Time
    MP 958; DP 1008; EP 963; NP 1046
    [OOR 1859, Rd 1924f & 2011f; Pr 634]

13. Thu. Thursday of the 28th Week in Ordinary Time
    MP 968; DP 1012; EP 973; NP 1049
    [OOR 1861, Rd 1924f & 2011f; Pr 634]

14. Fri. Weekday or St. Callistus I, Po & M (1289)
    MP (1414 or 1426) 978; DP 1017
    EP (1417 or 1430) 984; NP 1052
    [OOR 1864, Rd 1924f & 2011f or 2045f; Pr 1289 or 634]

15. Sat. St. Teresa of Avila, V & D (Mem) 1289
    MP (1435 or 1441) 988; DP 1022; EP (635) 701; NP 1034
    [OOR 1867, Rd 1924f & 2048f; Pr 1290]

16. **Sun. TWENTY-NINTH SUNDAY IN ORDINARY TIME 635**
    MP 706; DP 994; EP 712; NP 1037
    [OOR 1785, Rd 1924f & 2011f; TD Pr 635]

17. Mon. St. Ignatius of Antioch, B & M (Mem) 1291
    MP (1414 or 1426) (Ant) 718; DP 998
    EP (1417 or 1430) (Ant) 723; NP 1041
    [OOR 1788, Rd 1924f & 2045f; Pr 1292]

18. Tue. ST. LUKE, EVANGELIST (F) 1292
    MP 1293 (707); DP 1003; EP 1295 (1394); NP 1044
    [OOR 1791, Rd 1924f & 2043f; TD Pr 1294]

19. Wed. Sts. Isaac Jogues and John de Brébeuf, Pp & Mm, and Comps,
    Mm (Mem) 1297
    MP (1402 or 1426) 738; DP 1008; EP (1405 or 1430) 743; NP 1046
    [OOR 1794, Rd 1924f & 2045f; Pr 1297]

20. Thu. Weekday or St. Paul of the Cross, P (1297) **[transferred from 10/19]**
    MP (1426 or 1470) 748; DP 1012; EP (1430 or 1471) 754; NP 1049
    [OOR 1797, Rd 1924f & 2011f or 2046f; Pr 1298 or 635]

21. Fri. Friday of the 29th Week in Ordinary Time
    MP 759; DP 1017; EP 765; NP 1052
    [OOR 1800, Rd 1924f & 2011f; Pr 635]

22. Sat. Weekday or St. John Paul II, Po *(New)* (1426) or BVM on Saturday
    (1383)
    MP (1426) (1383) 770; DP 1022; EP (636) 775; NP 1034
    [OOR 1802, Rd 1924f & 2011f or 2046f or 1951f; Pr 1428 or 1386 or
    635]

23. **Sun. THIRTIETH SUNDAY IN ORDINARY TIME 636**
    MP 780; DP 994; EP 786; NP 1037
    [OOR 1806, Rd 1924f & 2011f; TD Pr 636]

24. Mon. Weekday or St. Anthony Claret, B (1299)
    MP (1426) 792; DP 998; EP (1430) 798; NP 1041
    [OOR 1809, Rd 1924f & 2011f or 2046f; Pr 1299 or 636]

25. Tue. Tuesday of the 30th Week in Ordinary Time
    MP 802; DP 1003; EP 807; NP 1044
    [OOR 1812, Rd 1924f & 2011f; Pr 636]

26. Wed. Wednesday of the 30th Week in Ordinary Time
    MP 812; DP 1008; EP 818; NP 1046
    [OOR 1816, Rd 1924f & 2011f; Pr 636]

27. Thu. Thursday of the 30th Week in Ordinary Time
    MP 824; DP 1012; EP 830; NP 1049
    [OOR 1819, Rd 1924f & 2011f; Pr 636]

28. Fri. STS. SIMON AND JUDE, AP (F) 1299
    MP 1392 (707); DP 1017; EP 1394; NP 1052
    [OOR 1821, Rd 1924f & 2043f; TD Pr 1300]

29. Sat. Weekday or BVM on Saturday (1383)
    MP (1383) 845; DP 1022; EP (637) 851; NP 1034
    [OOR 1824, Rd 1924f & 2011f & 1951f; Pr 1386 or 636]

30. **Sun. THIRTY-FIRST SUNDAY IN ORDINARY TIME 637**
    MP 856; DP 994; EP 861; NP 1037
    [OOR 1827, Rd 1924f & 2011f; TD Pr 637]

31. Mon. Monday of the 31st Week in Ordinary Time
    MP 867; DP 998; EP 1300; NP 1034
    [OOR 1829, Rd 1924f & 2011f; Pr 637]

NOVEMBER

1. **Tue. ALL SAINTS (Sol) 1304**
   MP 1304 (707); DP 1027; EP 1306; NP 1037
   [OOR 1831, Rd 1924f & 2036f or 2053f; TD Pr 1304)

2. Wed. ALL SOULS 1310
   MP 1486; DP 1493; EP 1497; NP 1037
   [OOR 1474, Rd 1478f & 2034f; Pr 1310]

3. Thu. Weekday or St. Martin de Porres, Rel (1310)
   MP (1470) (Ant) 897; DP 1012; EP (1471) (Ant) 901; NP 1049
   [OOR 1838, Rd 1924f & 2011f or 2049f; Pr 1311 or 637]

4. Fri. St. Charles Borromeo, B (Mem) 1311
    MP (1426) 906; DP 1017; EP (1430) 911; NP 1052
    [OOR 1842, Rd 1924f & 2046f; Pr 1312]

5. Sat. Weekday or BVM on Saturday (1383)
    MP (1383) 916; DP 1022; EP (638) 921; NP 1034
    [OOR 1845, Rd 1924f & 2011f or 1951f; Pr 1386 or 637]

6. **Sun. THIRTY-SECOND SUNDAY IN ORDINARY TIME 638**
    MP 925; DP 994; EP 931; NP 1037
    [OOR 1850, Rd 1924f & 2011f; TD Pr 638]

7. Mon. Monday of the 32nd Week in Ordinary Time
    MP 937; DP 998; EP 942; NP 1041
    [OOR 1853, Rd 1924f & 2011f; Pr 638]

8. Tue. Tuesday of the 32nd Week in Ordinary Time
    MP 947; DP 1003; EP 953; NP 1044
    [OOR 1856, Rd 1924f & 2011f; Pr 638]

9. Wed. DEDICATION OF ST. JOHN LATERAN (F) 1312
    MP 1360 (707); DP 1008; EP 1363; NP 1046
    [OOR 1859, Rd 1924f & 2011f; TD Pr 1362]

10. Thu. St. Leo the Great, Po & D (Mem) 1312
    MP (1426 or 1435) (Ant) 968; DP 1012
    EP (1430 or 1436) (Ant) 973; NP 1049
    [OOR 1861, Rd 1924f & 2046f; Pr 1313]

11. Fri. St. Martin of Tours, B (Mem) 1313
    MP 1314 (707); DP 1017; EP 1315 (1430); NP 1052
    [OOR 1864, Rd 1924f & 2046f; Pr 1315]

12. Sat. St. Josaphat, B & M (Mem) 1316
    MP (1414 or 1426) 988; DP 1022
    EP (639) 701; NP 1034
    [OOR 1867, Rd 1924f & 2045f; Pr 1317]

13. **Sun. THIRTY-THIRD SUNDAY IN ORDINARY TIME 639**
    MP 706; DP 994; EP 712; NP 1037
    [OOR 1785, Rd 1924f & 2011f; TD Pr 640]

14. Mon. Monday of the 33rd Week in Ordinary Time
    MP 718; DP 998; EP 723; NP 1041
    [OOR 1788, Rd 1924f & 2011f; Pr 640]

15. Tue. Weekday or St. Albert the Great, B & D (1318)
    MP (1426 or 1435) 728; DP 1003
    EP (1430 or 1436) 734; NP 1044
    [OOR 1791, Rd 1924f & 2011f or 2046f; Pr 1318 or 640]

16. Wed. Weekday or St. Margaret of Scotland (1319) or St. Gertrude, V (1319)
    MP (1472) (1441 or 1470) 738; DP 1008
    EP (1472) (1444 or 1471) 743; NP 1046
    [OOR 1794, Rd 1924f & 2011f or 2053f or 2048f; Pr 1319 or 1320 or 640]

17. Thu. St. Elizabeth of Hungary (Mem) 1320
    MP (1472) 748; DP 1012; EP (1472) 754; NP 1049
    [OOR 1797, Rd 1924f & 2053f; Pr 1320]

18. Fri. Weekday or Dedication of the Churches of Sts. Peter and Paul, Ap (1321) or St. Rose Philippine Duchesne, V **(New)** (26)
    MP (1392) (1441) (Ant) 759; DP 1017
    EP (1394) (1444) (Ant) 765; NP 1052
    [OOR 1800, Rd 1924f & 2011f or 2043f or 2048f; Pr 1321 or (27) or 1443 or 640]

19. Sat. Weekday or BVM on Saturday (1383)
    MP (1383) 770; DP 1022; EP 674; NP 1034
    [OOR 1802, Rd 1924f & 2011f or 1951f; Pr 1386 or 640]

20. **Sun. CHRIST THE KING (Sol) 677**
    MP 677 (707); DP 1027; EP 679; NP 1037
    [OOR 1806, Rd 1924f & 2011f; TD Pr 677]

21. Mon. Presentation of Mary (Mem) 1322
    MP (1372) (Ant) 792; DP 998; EP (1378) (Ant) 798; NP 1041
    [OOR 1809, Rd 1924f & 1951f; Pr 1322]

22. Tue. St. Cecilia, V & M (Mem) 1323
    MP (1414 or 1441) (Ant) 802; DP 1003
    EP (1417 or 1444) (Ant) 807; NP 1044
    [OOR 1812, Rd 1924f & 2045f or 2048f; Pr 1323]

23. Wed. Weekday or St. Clement I, Po & M (1324) or St. Columban, Ab (1324) or Bl. Miguel Agustín Pro, P & M **(New)** (27)

MP (1414 or 1426) (1426 or 1470) 812; DP 1008
EP (1417 or 1430) (1430 or 1471) 818; NP 1046
[OOR 1816, Rd 1924f & 2011f or 2045f or 2046f or 2049f; Pr 1324 or
    1325 or (28) or 1416 or 1429 or 640]

24. Thu. St. Andrew Dung-Lac, P, and Comps, Mm (Mem) **(New)** (28)
MP (1402) 824; DP 1012; EP (1405) 830; NP 1049
[OOR 1819, Rd 1924f & 2045f or (29); Pr (31) or 1404]

25. Fri. Weekday or St. Catherine of Alexandria, V & M *(New)* (1414 or
    1441)
MP (1414 or 1441) 835; DP 1017; EP (1417 or 1444) 840; NP 1052
[OOR 1821, Rd 1924f & 2011f or 2045f or 2048f; Pr 1417 or 1443 or
    640]

26. Sat. Weekday or BVM on Saturday (1383)
MP (1383) 845; DP 1022; EP (41) 701; NP 1034
[OOR 1824, Rd 1924f & 2011f or 1951f; Pr 1386 or 640]

27. Sun. **FIRST SUNDAY OF ADVENT 43**
MP (43) 706; DP 994; EP (45) 712; NP 1037
[OOR 1785, Rd 1870f & 1942f; TD Pr 44]

28. Mon. Monday of the 1st Week of Advent
MP (47) 718; DP 998; EP (48) 723; NP 1041
[OOR 1788, Rd 1870f & 1942f; Pr 48]

29. Tue. Tuesday of the 1st Week of Advent
MP (50) 728; DP 1003; EP (51) 734; NP 1044
[OOR 1791, Rd 1870f & 1942f; Pr 51]

30. Wed. ST. ANDREW, AP (F) 1325
MP 1325 (707); DP 1008; EP 1327 (1394); NP 1046
[OOR 1794, Rd 1870f & 2043f; TD Pr 1327]

DECEMBER

1. Thu. Thursday of the 1st Week of Advent
MP (56) 748; DP 1012; EP (57) 754; NP 1049
[OOR 1797, Rd 1870f & 1942f; Pr 57]

2. Fri. Friday of the 1st Week of Advent
MP (59) 759; DP 1017; EP (60) 765; NP 1052
[OOR 1800, Rd 1870f & 1942f; Pr 60]

3. Sat. St. Francis Xavier, P (Mem) 1329
   MP (1426) 770; DP 1022; EP (64) 775; NP 1034
   [OOR 1802, Rd 1870f & 2046f; Pr 1329]

4. **Sun. SECOND SUNDAY OF ADVENT 66**
   MP (66) 780; DP 994; EP (68) 786; NP 1037
   [OOR 1806, Rd 1870f & 1942f; TD Pr 67]

5. Mon. Monday of the 2nd Week of Advent
   MP (70) 792; DP 998; EP (72) 798; NP 1041
   [OOR 1809, Rd 1870f & 1942f; Pr 71]

6. Tue. Advent Weekday or St. Nicholas, B (1330)
   MP (1426) (73) 802; DP 1003; EP (1430) (74) 807; NP 1044
   [OOR 1812, Rd 1870f & 1942f or 2046f; Pr 1331 or 74]

7. Wed. St. Ambrose, B & D (Mem) 1331
   MP (1435) 812; DP 1008; EP 1332 (1368); NP 1034
   [OOR 1816, Rd 1870f & 2046f; Pr 1331]

8. **Thu. IMMACULATE CONCEPTION (Sol) 1334**
   MP 1334 (707); DP 1027; EP 1336 (1378); NP 1037
   [OOR 1819, Rd 1870f & 1951f; TD Pr 1336]

9. Fri. Advent Weekday or St. Juan Diego **(New)** (32)
   MP (1452) (82) 835; DP 1017; EP (1455) (83) 840; NP 1052
   [OOR 1821, Rd 1870f & 1942f or 2053f; Pr (33) or 1454 or 83]

10. Sat. Advent Weekday or Our Lady of Loreto *(New)* (1372)
    MP (1372) (85) 845; DP 1022; EP (87) 851; NP 1034
    [OOR 1824, Rd 1870f & 1942f or 1951f; Pr 86 or 39 in this Guide]

11. **Sun. THIRD SUNDAY OF ADVENT 89**
    MP (89) 856; DP 994; EP (91) 861; NP 1037
    [OOR 1827, Rd 1870f & 1942f; TD Pr 91]

12. Mon. OUR LADY OF GUADALUPE (F) **(New)** (33) or 1339
    MP (42) & 1372 (707); DP 998; EP (46) & 1378 Pr (48); NP 1041
    [OOR (33) & 1829, Rd 1870f & 1951f; TD Pr (42) or 1340]

13. Tue. St. Lucy, V & M (Mem) 1341
    MP (1414 or 1441) (Ant) 877; DP 1003
    EP (1417 or 1444) (Ant) 882; NP 1044
    [OOR 1831, Rd 1870f & 2045f or 2048f; Pr 1341]

14. Wed. St. John of the Cross, P & D (Mem) 1342
    MP (1435) 886; DP 1008; EP (1436) 892; NP 1046
    [OOR 1835, Rd 1870f & 2046f; Pr 1342]

15. Thu. Thursday of the 3rd Week of Advent
    MP (103) 897; DP 1012; EP (105) 901; NP 1049
    [OOR 1838, Rd 1870f & 1942f; Pr 104]

16. Fri. Friday of the 3rd Week of Advent
    MP (106) 906; DP 1017; EP (108) 911; NP 1052
    [OOR 1842, Rd 1870f & 1942f; Pr 108]

17. Sat. Saturday of the 3rd Week of Advent
    MP (116) 916; DP 1022; EP (110) 921 (Ant 118); NP 1034
    [OOR 1845, Rd 1870f & 1942f; Pr 117]

18. **Sun. FOURTH SUNDAY OF ADVENT 111**
    MP (112) 925 (Ant 119); DP 994; EP (114) 931 (Ant 121); NP 1037
    [OOR 1850, Rd 1870f & 1942f; TD Pr 113]

19. Mon. Monday of the 4th Week of Advent
    MP (122) 937; DP 998; EP (123) 942; NP 1041
    [OOR 1853, Rd 1870f & 1942f; Pr 123]

20. Tue. Tuesday of the 4th Week of Advent
    MP (125) 947; DP 1003; EP (126) 953; NP 1044
    [OOR 1856, Rd 1870f & 1942f; Pr 126]

21. Wed. Wednesday of the 4th Week of Advent
    MP (128) 958 (St. Peter Canisius, P & D 1343); DP 1008
    EP (129) 963 (St. Peter Canisius, P & D 1343); NP 1046
    [OOR 1859, Rd 1870f & 1942f; Pr 1343 or 129]

22. Thu. Thursday of the 4th Week of Advent
    MP (131) 968; DP 1012; EP (132) 973; NP 1049
    [OOR 1861, Rd 1870f & 1942f; Pr 132]

23. Fri. Friday of the 4th Week of Advent
    MP (134) 978 (St. John of Kanty, P 1344); DP 1017
    EP (136) 984 (St. John of Kanty, P 1344); NP 1052
    [OOR 1864, Rd 1870f & 1942f; Pr 1344 or 135]

24. Sat. Saturday of the 4th Week of Advent
    MP (137) 988; DP 1022; EP 140; NP 1034
    [OOR 1867, Rd 1870f & 1942f; Pr 139]

25. **Sun. CHRISTMAS (Sol) 144**
MP 144 (707); DP 1027; EP 147; NP 1034 or 1037
[OOR 1785, Rd 1882f & 1955f; TD Pr 146]

26. Mon. ST. STEPHEN, FIRST MARTYR (F) 1344
MP 1345 (707); DP 998; EP 147 & 159; NP 1034 or 1037
[OOR 1788, Rd 1882f & 1957f; TD Pr 1346]

27. Tue. ST. JOHN, AP & EVANGELIST (F) 1347
MP 1347 (707); DP 1003; EP 147 & 161; NP 1034 or 1037
[OOR 1791, Rd 1882f & 1959f; TD Pr 1348]

28. Wed. HOLY INNOCENTS, MM (F) 1349
MP 1349 (707); DP 1008; EP 147 & 162; NP 1034 or 1037
[OOR 1794, Rd 1882f & 1961f; TD Pr 1351]

29. Thu. FIFTH DAY IN THE OCTAVE OF CHRISTMAS
MP 144 & 164 (St. Thomas Becket, B & M 1352); DP 1012
EP 147 & 165 (St. Thomas Becket, B & M 1352); NP 1034 or 1037
[OOR 1797, Rd 1882f & 1955f; TD Pr 1352 or 165]

30. Fri. HOLY FAMILY (F) 154
MP 154 (707); DP 1017; EP 156 (1378); NP 1034 or 1037
[OOR 1800, Rd 1882f & 1955f; TD Pr 156]

31. Sat. SEVENTH DAY IN THE OCTAVE OF CHRISTMAS
MP 144 & 171 (St. Sylvester I, Po 1353); DP 1022
EP 173 (1368); NP 1034 or 1037
[OOR 1802, Rd 1882f & 1955f; TD Pr 1353 or 172]

Prayers

(For use on June 6, The Blessed Virgin Mary, Mother of the Church [Memorial])

O God, Father of mercies,
whose Only Begotten Son, as he hung upon the Cross,
chose the Blessed Virgin Mary, his Mother,
to be our Mother also,
grant, we pray, that with her loving help
your Church may be more fruitful day by day
and, exulting in the holiness of her children,
may draw to her embrace all the families of the peoples.
Through our Lord Jesus Christ, your Son,
who lives and reigns with you in the unity of the Holy Spirit,
God, for ever and ever.

(For use on December 10, Our Lady of Loreto [Optional Memorial])

O God, who, fulfilling the promise made to our Fathers,
chose the Blessed Virgin Mary
to become the Mother of the Savior,
grant that we may follow her example,
for her humility was pleasing to you
and her obedience profitable to us.
Through our Lord Jesus Christ, your Son,
who lives and reigns with you in the unity of the Holy Spirit,
God, for ever and ever.

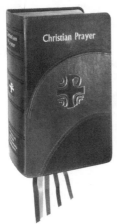

CHRISTIAN PRAYER

This regular-size edition of the official one-volume edition of the internationally acclaimed Liturgy of the Hours contains the complete texts of Morning and Evening Prayer for the entire year. With its readable 10-pt. type, ribbon markers for easy location of texts, and beautiful two-color printing, this handy volume simplifies praying the official Prayer of the Church for today's busy Catholic.

No. 406/19—Dura-Lux Binding **$46.00**
ISBN 978-1-941243-61-9

SHORTER CHRISTIAN PRAYER

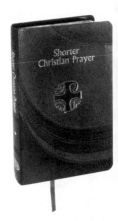

This abbreviated version of the internationally acclaimed Liturgy of the Hours contains Morning and Evening Prayer from the Four-Week Psalter and selected texts for the Seasons and Major Feasts of the year. Printed in two colors, this volume includes a useful ribbon marker. Its handy, practical size makes this edition ideal for parish use.

No. 408/19—Dura-Lux Binding **$22.00**
ISBN 978-1-941243-60-2

709/13

LITURGY OF THE HOURS

This is the official English edition of the Divine Office that contains the translation approved by the International Commission on English in the Liturgy.

No. 409/10 Set of 4 volumes.............................. **$159.00**
ISBN 978-0-89942-409-5

No. 409/13 Set of 4 volumes—Black Leather Binding
Note: available in sets only.................................. **$184.00**
ISBN 978-0-89942-411-8

No. 709/13 Set of 4 volumes—Large Print, Leather Binding. *Note: available in sets only*.................. **$207.00**
ISBN 978-0-89942-710-2

ACTUAL SIZE TYPE

READING

I know well the plans I have
Lord, plans for your welfare, n
you a future full of hope. When

409/10

409/13

41

A Companion to the Liturgy of the Hours:

Morning and Evening Prayer

By Shirley Darcus Sullivan

A spiritual companion for Morning and Evening Prayer of the Four-Week Psalter. It presents ways in which the experience of the Hours may be made more prayerful for those who say them, e.g., by using the spirituality of Carmel, especially that of Elizabeth of the Trinity. 208 pages. Size 5¹/₂ x 8¹/₄. Flexible full-color paper cover.

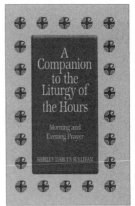

No. 415/04
ISBN: 978-0-89942-432-3
Price: $9.95

The Divine Office for Dodos

A Step-by-Step Guide to Praying the Liturgy of the Hours

By Madeline Pecora Nugent

For those who want to pray all the Hours correctly and completely, this book contains over 90 detailed lessons with questions, helpful hints, and practice sessions presented in a simple style. 272 pages. Size 5¼ x 7¾.

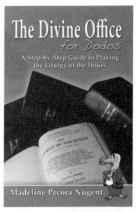

"There is hope in these pages! You are going to learn to pray the Divine Office! Honest! Then you will join the ranks of other clergy, religious, and laity, some of whom are non-Catholic, who pray the Divine Office every day."—From the Author's Introduction

No. 416/04
ISBN: 978-0-89942-482-8
Price: $9.95

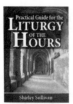

PRACTICAL GUIDE FOR THE LITURGY OF THE HOURS—By Shirley Sullivan. This book begins with a treatment of the two main Hours of Morning and Evening Prayer and then also presents the other Hours. It offers guidance to individuals as well as for groups to pray in a rich and meaningful way. 96 pages. Size 4³/₈ x 6³/₄.

No. 426/04—Flexible cover ISBN 978-0-89942-484-2 . . . . **$7.95**

COMPANION PRAYER BOOK TO THE LITURGY OF THE HOURS—By Georges-Albert Boissinot. This book is meant to help all clergy, religious, and lay people to share more fully in the Prayer of the Church through inspirational prayers and reflections centered on the celebration of the Hours. 128 pages. Size 4³/₈ x 6³/₄.

No. 434/04—Flexible cover ISBN 978-0-89942-354-8 . . . . **$8.95**

OTHER OUTSTANDING CATHOLIC BOOKS

HOLY BIBLE—The Saint Joseph Edition of the **NEW CATHOLIC BIBLE (NCB)** is a fresh, faithful, and reader-friendly translation. All editions are intended to be used by Catholics for daily prayer and meditation, as well as private devotion and group study. The editions feature Large, Readable Type, Rich Explanatory Notes, Maps, Photographs, a section entitled "Learning about Your Bible," and a Doctrinal Bible Index.

Family Edition	**No. 614**
Giant Type Edition	**No. 617**

NEW TESTAMENT—St. Joseph Edition of the **NEW CATHOLIC BIBLE** translation. Large, easy-to-read type, with helpful Notes and Maps. Features the words of Christ in red.

Vest Pocket Edition	**No. 650**
Study Edition—Includes many helps.	**No. 311**
Pocket Edition—Illustrated. (Christ's words not in red.)	**No. 630**

THE PSALMS—St. Joseph **NEW CATHOLIC BIBLE,** printed in large, easy-to-read type with copious informative notes and cross-references.

	No. 665

New St. Joseph

Handbook for Lectors & Proclaimers of the Word

Liturgical Year C — 2022

Rev. Jude Winkler, OFM Conv.

Unique and Valuable Features of This Catholic Book Publishing Edition:

✔ Contains the approved New American Bible text of the Readings for Sunday Mass (including Holy Thursday, Good Friday, and the Easter Vigil) for 2022.

✔ Helpful Commentary guides the lector or proclaimer of the Word to understand the context and background of the reading being proclaimed.

✔ Full text for each Mass, including the Responsorial Psalm and Alleluia Verse.

✔ Attractive Format—Each page has been very carefully arranged with optimum leading between lines and extra space between Readings.

No. 86/04
ISBN 978-1-953152-31-2
Price: $10.95

✔ Magnificently Illustrated—Over 60 liturgical drawings enhance the beauty of this text.

✔ Clear Running Heads show at a glance the date and title of every Sunday reading.

✔ Complete Text included for both longer and shorter forms of readings.

✔ Handy Index of Bible Texts enables lector or proclaimer to locate at a glance every Reading, Responsorial Psalm, or Alleluia Verse or Verse before the Gospel used during the current year.

✔ Helpful Short Glossary and Complete Pronunciation Guide

✔ Large Size: 8½ x 11

✔ Durable Binding

✔ Excellent Resource for RCIA Study Groups

OTHER OUTSTANDING CATHOLIC BOOKS

St. Joseph SUNDAY MISSAL—Complete Edition . . . in accord with *The Roman Misssal*, Third Edition. Includes all 3 Cycles (**A, B, and C**) with explanations. 1,600 pages. **No. 820**

St. Joseph WEEKDAY MISSAL (Vol. I & II)—All the Mass texts needed for weekdays in accord with *The Roman Misssal*, Third Edition. An indispensable aid for all who celebrate and participate at daily Mass.

Nos. 920 & 921

Large Type Edition **Nos. 922 & 923**

St. Joseph SUNDAY MISSAL—LARGE TYPE EDITION—Includes the Readings for the 3-year Cycle printed in extra-large type for easy reading. Includes full-color inserts. **No. 822**

St. Joseph CHURCH HISTORY—Sets forth the major events in the life of the Church in a clear and logical fashion that makes them understandable to the modern reader. Large type. Illustrated. **No. 262**

BIBLE MEDITATIONS FOR EVERY DAY—By Rev. John C. Kersten, S.V.D. Excellent aid for daily meditation. A Scripture passage and a short, invaluable introduction are given for every day. **No. 277**

MARY DAY BY DAY—Introduction by Rev. Charles G. Fehrenbach, C.SS.R. Minute Marian meditations for every day of the year, including a Scripture passage, a quotation from the Saints, and a concluding prayer. Over 300 illustrations in two colors. **No. 180**

NEW SAINT JOSEPH PEOPLE'S PRAYER BOOK—Edited by Rev. Francis Evans. An encyclopedia of prayers, drawn from the Bible and Liturgy, the *Enchiridion of Indulgences*, the Saints and spiritual writers—plus hundreds of traditional and contemporary prayers for every need. Over 1,400 prayers typeset in sense lines. Large type. Printed and illustrated in two colors. 1,056 pages. **No. 900**

FOLLOWING THE HOLY SPIRIT—By Rev. Walter van de Putte, C.S.Sp. Patterned after **The Imitation of Christ,** it contains dialogues with, and prayers to, the Holy Spirit. Large type. Illustrated. **No. 335**

MARY MY HOPE—By Rev. Lawrence G. Lovasik, S.V.D. Popular book of devotions to Mary. Large type. Illustrated. **No. 365**

catholicbookpublishing.com

catholicbookpublishing.com

The
LITURGY OF THE HOURS
is truly the prayer of the Church
for all the people of God —
bishops, priests, deacons,
religious and the
laity.

ISBN 978-1-953152-37-4

9 781953 152374   90000

This Guide is No. 406/G
ISBN 978-1-953152-37-4